THINGS MY STUDENTS SAID

A JOURNAL TO RECORD ACTUAL QUOTES THAT COME OUT OF YOUR STUDENTS' MOUTHS

THIS JOURNAL BELONGS TO:

Made in the USA
Columbia, SC
23 April 2022

59379582R00043